SECOND SKIN

KATERINA STOYKOVA

IC

Co-funded by the
Creative Europe Programme
of the European Union

Cover art by Luba Haleva
Design and typesetting by Asen Iliev
Copyright © 2019 Katerina Stoykova
Editor Nevena Dishlieva-Krysteva
Originally published in Bulgarian in 2018 by ICU

ISBN 978-619-7153-43-9

ICU
8 Hubavka Str
1111 Sofia, Bulgaria
icu-bg.com

Second

Skin

KATERINA STOYKOVA

*Translated from the Bulgarian
by the Author*

Sofia 2019

CONTENTS

How Are You Feeling, Child?

Welcome, Horror

that someone will read this
and realize you're worth nothing.
Decade after decade,
couldn't you get better?
Aren't you ashamed?
Oh, but you are.
Your mother insisted:
Don't tell anyone
your father beats us
Because they'll think
we did something
wrong to begin with.

8th Floor Balcony Ghazal

If I catch you smoking
I'll throw you off the balcony.

If something happens to you
I'll jump off the balcony.

Dad stopped hitting me: Go ahead, he laughed, scream for help.
Then opened the door to the balcony.

To free space in the kitchen,
we moved the stove to the balcony.

Dad got mad and started
dragging Mom towards the balcony.

You could see the sun rise
out of the Black Sea from the balcony.

When the guests for Mom's funeral arrived,
Dad hid, smoking on the balcony.

I hated him in the house,
as well as on the balcony.

I've been faking all my orgasms,
I confessed to my first ex-husband on the balcony.

I stared out for a month, waiting for my pen pal to arrive,
as I was scrubbing the windows on the balcony.

Your marriage will last at most three years,
Dad told me on the balcony.

When I was leaving for America, I looked up from the cab and saw
my best friend waving from the balcony.

I'm ready to let go of everything that happened
except the balcony.

Katerina, there is no heaven or hell,
there is just this balcony.

You Have the Right to Mourn, Dear One,

for not having a Daddy.
He sunk into the glass
and popped out
from time to time
to slap your face
during supper.
Good thing
you had already shut down
any feeling;
as much as possible,
you walked under water
from your room to the kitchen
while fearing the worst.
And your mother crooned:
The beast will kill us.
He will throw us off the balcony.
A part of me
is still falling downwards.
Another is clutching the rails,
like you, Mom, in the story you didn't keep to yourself:

When you had already moved out to live with Yuli, three days before the wedding, your father and I had an argument and he started dragging me to throw me off the balcony. I grabbed onto the door, otherwise who knows what'd have happened. I pretended that all was well so I wouldn't spoil your celebration.

I, too, pretended that all was well.

But it wasn't.
No, Mommy, no.

September 1971. I am exactly three months old. Mom and Dad, who live with my father's parents, take me to visit my mother's parents. They eat, hang out, then Grandma and Grandpa walk us to the bus stop. We wait. The bus is late. Then it arrives packed, and we can't get in. And there, at the bus stop, Grandpa turns to Grandma and tells her, *Take this kid to care for it!* By other accounts, Grandma says, *I should take this child!* Nobody speaks of my parents' reaction, but in a matter of minutes, the transfer is completed. They take the next bus without me.

So I could go back to work, was my mother's explanation. *We needed another paycheck.*

We were able to put a lot of money aside, bragged my father. *We saved your mother's entire salary. Every week we came for visitation. Sometimes twice a week. When you turned three, we tried to take you back, but we made you sick and gave you back to your grandparents until you turned six.*

Still, I had a crib at my parents' apartment and memories of a few visits.

If I had left you with them you would have died, said my grandmother once. Only once.

Why, I asked, but she just added, *They would have destroyed you,* and answered with silence to all follow-up questions.

I Couldn't Have Been More Than Four. I huddle at the back of my crib. I watch how my father tosses off the seventh-floor balcony everything we own – chairs, tables, shelves, books, the black-and-white TV. I don't make a sound, but my mother cries, *Don't, Yanko, don't*. A neighbor rings the doorbell. My father answers armed with a giant screwdriver, *Get out of here or I'll stab you*. The neighbor disappears. I don't remember what happens next. For years the residents of the Izgrev neighborhood discuss that crazy guy who threw all his belongings off the balcony.

We move to another apartment.

Slaveikov neighborhood. Block 55.

Eighth floor.

Welcome, Fear-of-My-Father.

It's time to take you out
and drape you on the line.
Second skin, I see you.

Here Is What I Remember. Saturday or Sunday. Lunchtime. Dad is running late. Mom is getting mad. She decides she's waited too long, we get dressed in nice clothes, put on shoes, and as we're about to go out, my father appears at the door.

Where are you going? He asks.

Out. Mom answers defiantly.

You're not going anywhere!

This I clearly remember. From that point on they start yelling and I don't understand everything, because I'm four. Dad orders me to go to the kitchen, and I do, but Mom is screaming and crying, and I tiptoe back quietly, and see them on the floor. She is on her back, he's sprawled on top of her. I make a noise to interrupt them. My father doesn't hear, but I inch closer until my mother sees me, speaks something in Dad's ear, he gets up, grabs me, carries me under his armpit and locks me in the kitchen.

I sit there, stare at my shoes, and listen to my mother's screams.

For days after that, she doesn't get out of bed. Her head sinks into the pillow. Her white pants are ripped to pieces. Grandma tends to her and mumbles curses about *that beast*. I quietly play and observe.

Then Mom and Dad divorce.

For about 10 months.

Years after that I was slammed with the memory and horror of these scenes. I didn't know that psychiatrists call them flashbacks. As I'd play, suddenly I'd find myself among the violence and would live it again. Then I'd run to my parents and say:

Dad, I almost forgot about that time you beat up Mom.

They'd just look at me without saying anything, until once Mom scolded me that I shouldn't speak of such things.

So I never mentioned it again.

But didn't forget it, either.

How Are You Feeling, Child?
Endangered. As a species.

How Are You Feeling, Child?
Like a rock travelling through the air.

How Are You Feeling, Child?
Like the stick left over
from the lollipop.

**Welcome, Feeling-
That-You've-Lost-Something,**

yet you're not sure
you want to find it again.
Welcome, tunnel
to some other self.

Welcome, Pain-of-Abandonment.

Move through me, feel free
to expand, claim
the spaces you need.
Balloon in my stomach.
Sometimes I think
you are me.

The Six-Year-Old Girl Told Her Father She Didn't Love Him.

It was a fine, unusually calm Saturday. They had just finished eating the food the mother had served for lunch. The TV was on.

Dad, I don't love you. I don't love you at all, the girl said. She didn't think that he'd care, but he got very upset.

He yelled, *I am leaving this house. I won't stay in a place where people don't love me,* and without hitting anyone, he slammed the door and disappeared for the afternoon, despite his wife's crying and his daughter's confused, contradictory apologies.

Hello, Horror-With-No-Name.

You stand
pressed to the wall
in the shade.
I cannot describe you
nor call you forward.
I can only love you
for I think you, too, are afraid.
Now that we are together
maybe it won't be so bad.

At the Hospital

How are you feeling, Mom?
They'll keep me here for a while.

What did you tell the doctors?
I told them that I fell.

Dad is waiting outside. He asks
if you would like to see him.

Of course. Please send him in.

Grandma Interrogates

Why is your mother in the hospital?
I don't know. She got sick.

Did your father beat her?
No.

What did he do to her this time? Tell me the truth.
No.

May the plague strike dead this beast.

Dad, Do You Remember,

the relatives from the village came to visit
us in the city and, as a gift, brought us a live chicken.

For days, the doomed thing lived
behind the bathroom door, its legs tied in a knot.

You refused to kill it.
I can't, you said.

Sewn with Flaming Threads. The glass full of fire. Some thing confused with another. What replaced with anything. Slap presenting itself as a kick. A question pretending to be love. What do I want to be free of? Let's start with years of my life. Preferably the ones to come. It's hard to believe I've wanted this life. Chosen my father. Waited to land in my mother's womb, and there, whole for the first time, started to divide.

Sewn in Like a Body in a Bag, Ancient

like myself, my dolls –
my childhood toys – arrive
from Bulgaria by airplane.

With crumpled hair, detached retinas,
ears nearly ripped off, they take as much
space as they did before.

Now what, they ask me condescendingly.
We'll live together, I answer persuasively.

Tour of the House

TEDDY

In 1973 he and I fell in love. I remember the toy store being closed, Dad and I staring through the window, the first time I was asked to choose whatever I'd like.

The big bear, I say.

Think well, Dad warns, but at two, I hadn't yet been taught to second-guess myself.

Then one day Teddy appears, and he becomes my closest companion. We are the same size. I dress him up in my clothes. We wrestle, and I win, for the most part. We drink tea, slow dance the way I've seen my parents do on good days.

Forty years later his wooly chest still makes a grunt whenever I lean him forward or pat his back to shake off the dust.
His right ear has come undone.

LILLY

I got her during the year my parents lived apart. Mom didn't talk a lot then, just said she was the one who bought the toys, not Santa. I asked what about the other kids, and she answered they also got presents from their parents and then for the first time I knew what it was like to become aware of the existence of a worldwide lie.

Lilly was beautiful. I could braid and unbraid her dark hair and put her to sleep. Mom sewed a purple dress around her body.

I couldn't take it off without ripping it, so I didn't. Even now, when the fabric is falling apart.

THE BABY

My parents brought her from the exotic country of East Germany. After they got back together and before we moved out of the studio apartment, they went on an international excursion throughout the countries allowed: Romania, Poland, Hungary, The Soviet Union…

The Baby never got a name. I tried many, but none felt real. She had the skill of peeing on herself. She could actually drink milk, and then, if you squeezed her leg, you'd have to change her.

For a while, the Baby was my favorite. I took her with me whenever I went to visit Grandma, or if Mom and I had to run away for a few days.

THE CAT

The cat is blue, lanky, has needed a bath for at least 20 years. I had stopped playing with toys in favor of boys when my mother brought me this gift. Tommy, I named him, after another cat my father kicked out for sitting on his seat.

The first time I got married, I was twenty. The photographer didn't know he was shooting with a faulty camera. Only four pictures survived.

One – me in my room, sitting in my writing chair, Tommy lying across my lap.

In the rest of the photos I'm alone. Although in my womb, in his third lunar month, glows my son.

Pippi

Red hair, dress with patches, big toothy smile. Loved her dearly. I read the book in one continuous loop, imagining I could be this strong and nobody would hit me and remain unpunished.

Thirty years later I heard that we build our lives to reenact our favorite childhood tale.

Mother – an angel in heaven.

Dad – living alone somewhere.

A girl with superhuman strength who doesn't need anything.

Construction Set

I built entire neighborhoods, high-rise after high-rise, streets, trains, playgrounds. Few generals have toppled more cities than I built from age four.

Mom, look, I'd say, and she'd turn and light up: *Very nice,* then dip back into her conversation with Vesselina, who kindly brought us bread and pork fat for dinner.

You'll grow up to be an architect, Mom said, but I didn't.

You'll grow up to be an architect, I told my son, and he did.

Welcome, Yearning-to-Die.

Oh, how familiar we are.
We've stalked each other since youth,
we've retched on mother's milk.
Used to play dolls –
those who shut their eyes
and never breathe.
Do you remember
I'd inhale
and swear
I wouldn't exhale?
There, on that chair
I still have – a monument
to an unforgotten era.
You carved a home
under my ribs.
From time to time you crack
the door to the balcony.
Yes, I know
on which floor we live.

The Kiss Goodnight

Every night, the same thing. He sat by the door with his glass of rakia. The girl, at the bottom of the room schemed, visualized walking out of the room without giving her father a goodnight kiss. He insisted on his kiss, one of the privileges of working heavy labor – *like a slave,* he liked to say – he worked too hard for her, to not get a kiss.

Every night the stress of getting up, walking past and opening the door to the dark corridor.

More often than not she went ahead and kissed him.

At times she omitted, and he called her back.

On a few occasions he didn't notice, but never two nights in a row; her hopes of making a new habit of not kissing goodnight – shattered.

Another feeling she had to disconnect from every day.

She mastered the autopilot.

Getting up, walking up to her father, shutting down, leaning in, kissing his cheek even though she wanted him dead, then good night and go to bed. The angry layer traveling through her like a jellyfish through water until it hits a wall.

She hated having to love him. Hated having to pretend, act as if, force herself to, felt guilty when she couldn't, felt a fraud, even though she didn't know the word yet, she felt wrong, both mistaken and a mistake. There must be some reason, there must be some good reason, some forgotten feeling, some thing that could counter her desire for him to die, her yearning for the relief of his being gone. Oh, she hated him but forced herself to love him, and she failed but managed to learn to hate herself. That, she learned well.

Three Incidents

1.
Apply face cream, then pat a layer of powder.
Then more cream and more powder
until you can't see it anymore.
My mother, camouflaging my bruises before I went to
school.

2.
You wash blood with cold water, my father scolded me.
He stood behind me by the sink and oversaw
that I correctly rinsed the blood running from my nose.
I know, I replied and stared back at his eyes in the mirror.

3.
The yelling was over.
My cheeks burned with tears
and handprints.
Strange... I thought, *I can't feel anything.*
I must be getting stronger.

Hit and Tell Villanelle

My mother told my father's friend,
He beats us both and treats us bad.
My father didn't hit and tell.

The friend was rather shocked, I guess
Dad must have felt a little bad.
My mother told my father's friend.

Dragan sat silent, shook his head,
Mom kept telling on my dad.
My father didn't hit and tell.

Mom spoke a lot, perhaps she felt
Dragan to be her friend, as well.
My mother told my father's friend.

I only listened, but I drank this man's
disgusted wrath and outrage.
My father didn't hit and tell.

In the end, though, nothing changed.
No one did a thing to help.
My mother told my father's friend.
My father didn't hit and tell.

I Love You, Refusal-to-Feel.

I want to feel you.
I see your back –
dignified.
Your hands –
occupied.
They lather foam.
You're about
to shave your face.
The razor shudders,
I hear the sound
of the blade.
Each stroke – deliberate,
studied.
When you're finished
you'll present
a clean,
smiling face.

How Are You Feeling, Child?
Scorched with self-loathing.

How Are You Feeling, Child?
As if I've nursed on blood.

How Are You Feeling, Child?
Flying from one abyss to another.
Don't want to jump off the balcony
but I am waiting to die.

One Afternoon Again I came back from school and Dad again returned from work and again started yelling, but this time I swallowed all aspirin in the house and began waiting to die. And when my ears started ringing, I got scared and called my mother, who flew in from work and made me drink compote and stick my fingers down my throat a few times. I drank. I puked. Can't remember what kind of compote that was – either strawberries or white cherries. She ordered me to not tell anyone, because they'd lock me up in the madhouse. I can't recall what else she said, but I remember feeling ashamed. During dinner, my father muttered they loved me very much. The incident was never brought up again, except by my mother's best friend, who cautioned me to take pity on my mother and spare her worries.

One Day, after the Last Class, my teacher – Comrade Paskaleva – called me to her desk, and said:

Katerina, I want to ask you something. Why are you always sad? You are always sad. Why?

It was as though I'd been zapped by electricity. I was astounded that someone wanted to know how I felt. I looked at her dumbfounded.

Think about it, she said. *And tell me.*

Ok, I agreed.

It was Friday evening. I started thinking. Thought all weekend, as well as on Monday, because I had class with her on Tuesday. Didn't tell my parents. Don't remember what I came up with for an answer, but I knew I was ready to share it with her. Went to class. My heart fluttered. I sought her eyes. She didn't act as if she expected a conversation. The class ended. I waited for her to call me to her, but she didn't. And I realized – she had forgotten. Or no longer cared to know.

Mommy, Mommy,

How we'd run away from home
whenever Dad kicked us out
or it got too dangerous.
How I wanted to protect you,
how we scurried together
almost folded in half,
how we cowered
in the attics of nearby high-rises,
and then at grandma's for a while,
or at your friend Zhenya's
with Natashka and Hristo,
until things calmed down,
until Dad started apologizing
and you began reciting
justifications and allowances:
Because, other than that, he really loves us.
And because, other than that, he works hard.
And gives up his entire salary.
And doesn't run around.
There are men who constantly cheat.
Do you know how bad that is?
I don't know, Mommy,
yet again I dismissed
the person next to me
and I'm still alone.

Welcome, Moment

you look into a mirror
and on its frame
you notice seven roses,
painted.
At least five of them look open
as if screaming in horror.
Their mouths have teeth.
How disturbed do you have to be
to see this?
Your second ex-husband said
You are damaged
and you agreed.
Two of the roses resemble
regular flowers.
Although one of them has
its head hanging downwards.

Thank You, Suspicion

that nobody loves you.
And how could they,
since they understand,
since you too see yourself
and what you're worth.
What are you worth?
Really! I want to know.
Didn't your own mother
pridefully tell you
to be aware
of your own value.

Welcome, Jealousy.

Your wild body spirals.
Bristles sprout.
Tusks thrust through the cheeks,
burst out.

Welcome, Jealousy,

the jolt
that leaves you petrified.
This flaming tide
would feel tight and snug,
if it didn't burn you alive.

How Are You, Child?

Wherever I go, I bring my own prison. My restrictions are animate. And hazardous. And all-encompassing. Reflective of my past like a rearview mirror. I can talk to someone and, without asking, surmise what kind of parents she's had. And those mastering spiritual practices I can spot with the naked eye. And those in need of therapy. And those who can't manage their own lives, and those who shun the truth, because it's too much.

At the Bottom

of Mom's purse
lay an envelope
with secret money
in case Dad kicked us out,
in case we ran off,
or home became dangerous
or Mom decided she wanted
some fashionable coat
with two rows of buttons in front
or a pink dress
with slender strings and a fancy pocket,
or original Italian shoes
with bows and amber ornaments,
or earrings, earrings, earrings,
hoops, pendants, trinkets,
necklaces – from plastic-cheap to boutique,
and shirts and skirts,
store bought, tailored, imported,
appeared as if by magic,
and both of us sported them.
Didn't Mom always say:
You have no taste,
you have no clue
how to put together an outfit.

And I wore your clothes, Mom.
Loved to look like you, all beautiful.

Welcome, Disappointment.

I feel you, Loneliness –
a child walled in
a well,
water reaching her chest.
You look up.
There is nobody.
The pail has been lowered,
but what could that help?

I Love You, Conditioned Reflex. I Love You,

Leap-back-to-the-unhappiness,
your warm familiarity feeling familial.
It should. You are its mother. And its father.
Its food and its stomach.

**Welcome, Feeling-
of-Being-Defeated.**

It took awhile
but here 'tis now –
boring busy life
you don't know
how to fight
from this point on
you've lost the sense of
what you wanted
to keep alive.

Having Destroyed Her Life,

she pushed further.
I don't expect
you'd understand,
she said
to no one.
There was nobody left.
If she could have,
she would have
fled herself
fast and away.
She knew
there was no good
to be had
by sticking to her.
With her?
Who was she anyway?
She didn't want to know
or be her.

That much was clear
for years
to anyone
who came near.
At least I wrote a poem,
she thought,
then didn't know
what to do
or avoid doing.
Thus the story ends.

P.S.
Then she burst
in flames
and all was well.

Welcome, Aggression-Towards-Yourself.

How the fuck did we get here,
how can we get away?
Give me one good line
of poetry
to make this worthwhile
then crawl back to hell.

Mommy, Mommy, Mommy, Mommy

you loved being pretty
for a fancy haircut
you'd sell your soul
you took me to the salon
that famous stylist
rubbed his dick on my ass
while he cut my hair
casually caressed my breasts
even squeezed a little bit
almost as if by mistake
Mom, he touches, I told you

Yes, he does, you shrugged

Mom, he touches, I told you
almost as if by mistake
even squeezed a little bit
casually caressed my breasts
while he cut my hair
rubbed his dick on my ass
that famous stylist
you took me to the salon
you'd sell your soul
for a fancy haircut
you loved being pretty
Mommy, Mommy, Mommy, Mommy

Hello, Outrage

I don't know
where you come from
but I see
your thorny skin
spiraling underneath mine.
Two bracelets
on the same wrist.
Turning
in opposite ways.
I watch, wait
for this to end.
Your anger
makes love to mine.
One of us understands
the other
won't be able
to survive.

How Are You Feeling, Child?
As if within wax.

How Are You Feeling, Child?
Like a sock turned inside out.

How Are You Feeling, Child?
Stranger to my own self.

"I Haven't Had a Single Good Day in My Life" – Mom

As soon as I moved in with him, he started hitting me, but I stayed because I was already pregnant with you. I had a terrible pregnancy. You were a difficult birth. Because of you I married your father again. You didn't have a coat. And he bought you a coat. Because of you I stay with him. So you have a father. I live because of you. If it weren't for you, I'd jump off the balcony.

No, Mommy. No. No. No.

How Are You Feeling, Child?
Unclean. Alone.

What Can I Do for You, Child?
You can jump off the balcony.

(Although I can, I actually can. No need to wait for someone else to do it. I leap, fly through the air, see everything from above, land in front of my schoolmate Lilly's auto parts store. My head shatters on the staircase, like a soft-boiled egg, and whatever was inside, is finally free to flee. My guts – wrapped around the ankles. Two vultures fly in and peck at my eyes. A wolf gnaws on my arm. Ravens dig through the heart. Neighbors scream and pull their hair. Someone calls 911 and says no need to rush. Meanwhile I ascend and soar. Before I could rise so high, first I needed to collapse. But isn't it always like that? My poor body, breathless and immobile, forgive me, I am sorry. I've set sail for nowhere, and there bodies aren't welcome. Only the insides of the insides turn up in the soup of hades, where I'm slurped into the ladle of some random demon, and I flow into his body – stubbly and crimson. And, believe me if you will, I start feeling better.)

How Are You Feeling, Child?
Ashamed to think all that.

Welcome, Fear-of-Fear.

We meet again.
We need again.
We hide together.

One Day I Got So Mad,

I almost
hit my mother.

She leaned back, cornered to the wall,
eyes wide with surprise

and fear. I was, in fact,
much stronger. After her

three years of growing cancer,
liver bulging like a baby bump,

there was no doubt
who would be the winner.

I can't remember what she'd said
to make me flip,

but I cannot forget
helping her lie back in bed

after that.

Last Trip to the Movies

We asked her where she'd been.
She said she'd gone to see
the new Eddie Murphy movie.

I asked you to take me,
but you never found the time.

We watched her from the balcony.

With small, careful steps
she was returning home
with nobody's help.

By My Mother's Grave
the shell of a snail.

Conversation

Daddy, why is your face so sad?
Because your Mommy died, baby.

Why do you visit the grave every day, Daddy?
Baby, she's there every day.

Daddy, your pillow is bitter with salt.
Is that a question, baby?

When Mom Died

and I left
for America,

he lived alone
for thirteen years.

Then he bought
a little yellow canary

to make noise at home.
The bird died as soon as

my father began adoring it.
That's it! He told me

over the phone.
No more living things.

Once

she got mud on her shoes
and never wore them again.

Many times
when she was little
her father hit her,
so when she left home
she never called him again.

(Well, almost.
Called every week
but loving him
was difficult.)

Welcome, Loneliness.

You and I
make one.

Priceless Advices

For my parents

Don't leave
        your donkey in the mud. Never
pity a man. Don't let the boys touch
from the waist down.
Don't look
        for strawberry seeds
in the shit. Whatever you do,
you do unto yourself.
Sleep well, you won't get away
with anything.

Black Stone Over White Stone
After Cesar Vallejo

I will die in Bourgas, under the pouring rain
that falls once a year
or two, whenever I can visit.
I will die on the eighth-floor balcony, at sunrise
as the sky tugs the sun's soul out
of the Black Sea shimmer.

It will be a Friday, as it is today,
because as I write these lines, I notice
how the work week ends and how
I crawl into another
pile – unfinished business.

Katerina died – during her visit.
Whoever is returning to Kentucky
isn't she, believe me. Determined
to remain unnoticed, this person mirrors
her disappearing foreign bones completely.

The only witnesses remain
the balcony, the rain,
the constant resurrections.

We Must Be Very Careful When Using the Word *Home.*

At home, at our apartments.
Two kilometers on foot
from the cemetery and
our mothers' rectangles. At home,

where it's tragic and filled
with our own existence. At home,
we can find honey, mint tea,
know everyone's secrets. At home

we suspect our neighbors.
We do not spit in the elevator. We
receive letters. We may be in love,
or may not be. That doesn't matter.
We are, and love is. At home

there is an old, reddish chair on which
we wrote our first poem. At home
every object is owned
by an emotion.

Time has stopped as if everything
were waiting to see us. At home –
that means we've been needed. At home –
a record number of ghosts.

One dresses our wounds, another – a salad,
third asks about living abroad – he also wants
to see where his happiness lies.

There is more. We only have to pull
open a drawer. We take items out,
put them back, close –
stairs from ourselves we've climbed, for which
there is no space
where we live, but we can still keep
at home.

Once I Opened the Door

to my parents' bedroom
and saw them kissing
as if they loved each other
as if they wanted one another
as if they were happy
to be together.
I was astounded, because
only an hour before
Mom had spoken to me again
of how bad he was,
what terrible things he did,
how she wished we could leave.
And so, only an hour before
she had lanced the next
consecutive blade of hate
in the field of my loathing,
where, after all,
I ended up alone.
She was in his arms,
her breasts – bare,
and she lay on top
like someone starting to play.
Didn't appear to hate him.

And maybe she didn't.

Welcome, Pain-of-Loss.

This emptiness
yearns to be filled with something.
Give yourself time –
you will invent things unimaginable.
Now, no need to contemplate.
Don't feed this ache
aggressively,
exhaustively,
beforehand.

How Are You Feeling, Child?
Smeared like butter on bread.

How Are You Feeling, Child?
You don't want to know.

How Are You Feeling, Child?
I don't want to know either.

Welcome, Unfamiliar Knocking

on the heart or in the heart. Or of it.
In any case, something perseveres.
Everyone's holding their breath,
but nobody closes the distance.

Welcome, Aggression,

where did you come from?
I see you've travelled some distance.
Your feet – bare.
Your mouth – sneering.
Do you have something to say?
I see you shaking with rage,
waiting for the day to end
before you kick the dog
or cast aside the one
who by some merciful miracle
is still sticking with you.
Yes, it is clear
you're not especially clever.
Miserable bitch,
only you are this broken.
The others seem normal.
They sing and drink,
laugh and photograph.
You better hide
and beat yourself up.

Hello, Self-Loathing,

let's shake hands.
You refuse to touch me?
I completely understand.

A Decade After Mom Died, I Destroyed the Documents from the Court Doctor.

She took me there. We went early and waited in line with a group of somber Gypsies. When we saw the doctor, turned out he and my mother knew one another.

Matushka, what are you doing here? He asked, and she started crying and explaining what a bad husband she had.

Then the nurse measured our bruises with a ruler.

And the lump behind Mom's ear.

They described everything in forms and handed her papers to use in a potential divorce hearing. She didn't get that far because Dad promised again that he would stop acting like this.

Is he her real father? The doctor asked.

Yes.

Dream. My father and I, facing each other. We eat. At the table. I thank him for something, and he laughs so violently, that his dentures start slipping out of his mouth. I see teeth under the teeth. *Your dentures are loose,* I warn him. He pushes them back. Then asks:

Katerina, have I ever been a father to you?

I think for a second, then say:

Yes.

I startle and wake up.

The First Time I Tried to Talk About My Childhood, my father shut the space and stated that for everything there must have been a reason. He slammed the door on the conversation I had practiced for months. I had flown across the ocean, tried the words before a mirror, gathered strength, wore amulets, but maybe I shouldn't have begun with a lie:

Dad, I forgive you for beating me and Mom.

Where did that come from? He exclaimed, and his face turned dark.

"It's Not True! Your Mother Has Never Stayed in a Hospital!" – Dad

The second time I tried to discuss my childhood was over Skype. My father and I were yelling at each other, after I hadn't called for two years.

I wanted to talk, to cry. I wanted him to say he was sorry.

Not only was he surprised, but it turned out he'd forgotten everything.

Tell me one bad thing I've done to you or your mother! He challenged me.

No, Daddy. No, no, no.

"He Lives as if the Past Doesn't Exist" – Katerina

He lives as if
the past doesn't exist.
I live as if
the past hasn't passed.
Mom passed.
At 47 years.
Dad lives as if
Mom doesn't exist.
I live as if
Mom isn't past.
The past has passed.
At 47 years.

The Wooden Spoon

My mother cooked with it
       & when she got sick
I cooked with it
       & when I left
my father cooked with it
       & when I came back
       for a brief visit
       to see
if I could
love him
       still

I took the spoon

       & I haven't
       cooked since.

Dad,

I dream
that I love you.

I dream
we stroll

together
by the sea shore.

The waves stretch out
and withdraw

don't reach us
but go on.

We keep
silent

a safe distance
apart.

I Love You, Loneliness,

sweet cliché
wrapped in yellowed newspaper
featuring a photo of you
when things were supposed
to get better.
You may have made
a step ahead, even two,
though the Earth
under you
switched direction.

I Love You, Alarm Clock,

for working to wake up
the one who has left
the room or fallen
asleep elsewhere
or gone deaf
through the night
or drowned
taking a bath
or decided he wanted
to listen to the alarm.
One way or another
nobody presses THE END.
Anxiety seeps
into space.
I love you, Alarm Clock.
You do your job well.
Those reluctant to awake
salute you.

Dream in Nepal

My father was dropping me off at the airport, I was about to travel to some distant place. I rummaged through my backpack looking for my glasses, and eventually found them, broken.

Give them to me, I'll fix them, offered my father.

I refused.

I want to buy new ones, I insisted, and discarded the damaged glasses.

The door to the airplane was open and waiting. I started running towards my gate. Then I remembered I hadn't hugged my father goodbye and clearly felt how my heart regretted it. I stopped and rushed back calling out: *Dad, Dad.* He was walking away slowly but heard me and turned around.

I didn't want to leave before I gave you a hug, I told him, embraced him and recognized his gratitude for my unedited act of warmth. Then right there, in my dream, without barriers and prejudice, as I was holding him, I was able to feel my love expand. The energy whirled from and around me. Tears rose with the tide and I wept in my sleep. That's how I woke up and remembered everything.

Yes, You Will Be Given

the strength you ask for,
but first the water
will test its dam.
The wind will hollow
the willow,
self-pity will push
away kindness.
There will be no others
to help.
Yes, you will get
the strength you ask for,
after we see
where you break
fall, get up,
break, fall,
get up,
not break.

Welcome, Feeling-of-Well-Being.

You surprised me this morning.
A rainbow of joy
sans the pot of gold.
Clearing through your healing.
Remember. It is possible.
Don't let me tell you
there is no hope.

Praise Song for the Wound

praise this wound
opening and closing
like a mouth
like a flower
like a pond
and its ice
praise this wound
opening and closing
like a womb
praise this wound's
resilience
its unpredictable
autoimmune wisdom
knowing when to bloom
when to shroud
praise its beauty
and the distance
it's made me travel
praise this wound
opening and closing
like a clam
praise its stubborn
pearl of healing
praise this wound
opening and closing
like a jaw
like a trap

praise its firm grip
opening and closing
like the fist
of the heart
like a door
to the past
a packaged gift
the outrage
of not having grown
any happier
the surprise
that you've been caught
by surprise
at its opening and closing
a step ahead of me
a step away from you
then another step
then another

Katerina Stoykova is both author and translator of *Second Skin*, as well as the author of several other poetry books in English and Bulgarian. The Bulgarian edition of *Second Skin* (*ICU*, 2018, Bulgarian) received wide acclaim and was awarded a grant from the European Commission's program *Creative Europe* to be translated and published in English.

Katerina's poetry collection *How God Punishes* came out in English in 2017 from *Broadstone Books*. The Bulgarian version of this book was published in 2014 by *ICU press* and won the *Ivan Nikolov National Poetry Prize*.

Katerina is the editor and main translator of *The Season of Delicate Hunger: Anthology of Contemporary Bulgarian Poetry* (*Accents Publishing*, 2014). For six years Katerina hosted the literary radio show *Accents* on WRFL 88.1FM, Lexington and recorded hundreds of hours of conversations with poets and writers from the USA and around the world. In 2010, Katerina launched the independent literary press *Accents Publishing*. The press publishes predominantly poetry collections and recently launched a printed magazine, *Literary Accents*.

Katerina acted the lead roles in the independent feature films *Proud Citizen* and *Fort Maria*, both directed by Thom Southerland. Additionally, Katerina was the co-writer for *Proud Citizen*. The film received a number of festival awards, including two special acting awards for Katerina's performance.

Last but not least, Katerina is a proud graduate of the Spalding Master of Fine Arts in Writing program.

.

Acknowledgements

Heartfelt gratitude to the wonderful literary press ICU and its team of superheroes. Nevena Dishlieva-Krysteva, Ivo Krystev, Luba Haleva, Asen Iliev and Iva Koleva, thank you for the care and time you dedicated to this book and what it stands for. Thank you to all who read and provided feedback at various stages of this manuscript in Bulgarian and/or English.
The following poems are included in both English and Bulgarian as voiceovers in the independent film *Proud Citizen*:
The Six-Year-Old Girl Told Her Father She Didn't Love Him.
One Day
Last Trip to the Movies

I am grateful to the editors of the magazines in which these poems first appeared:
Dad, Do You Remember, the Relatives in Diode Editions, Volume 6, Summer 2013
Hit and Tell Villanelle in Snakeskin 226: February 2016
Conversation in Poetry International, issue 22/23, 2017
Black Stone Over White Stone in Nebo, fall 2015 issue, Vol. 34 No. 1.

Deep gratitude to the European Commission for their support in the translation, publication and promotion of this book.

www.ingramcontent.com/pod-product-compliance
Lightning Source LLC
Chambersburg PA
CBHW071536120626

46550CB00006B/2474

* 9 7 8 6 1 9 7 1 5 3 4 3 9 *